Date: 6/7/16

J 631.55 PET
Pettiford, Rebecca,
Harvesting /

WAY TO GROW! GARDENING
HARVESTING

by Rebecca Pettiford

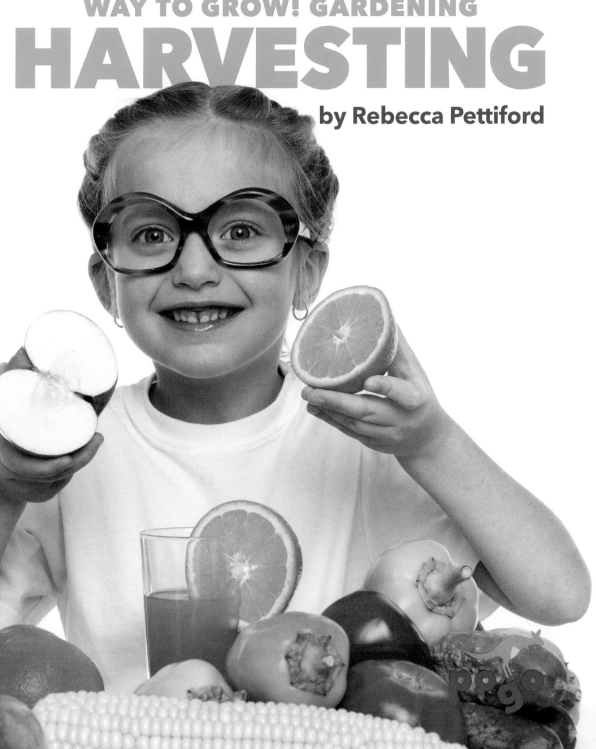

Ideas for Parents and Teachers

Pogo Books let children practice reading informational text while introducing them to nonfiction features such as headings, labels, sidebars, maps, and diagrams, as well as a table of contents, glossary, and index.

Carefully leveled text with a strong photo match offers early fluent readers the support they need to succeed.

Before Reading

- "Walk" through the book and point out the various nonfiction features. Ask the student what purpose each feature serves.
- Look at the glossary together. Read and discuss the words.

Read the Book

- Have the child read the book independently.
- Invite him or her to list questions that arise from reading.

After Reading

- Discuss the child's questions. Talk about how he or she might find answers to those questions.
- Prompt the child to think more. Ask: Have you ever picked berries from a bush or apples from a tree? Did you eat the fruit right away? Or did you use it to make something else?

Pogo Books are published by Jump!
5357 Penn Avenue South
Minneapolis, MN 55419
www.jumplibrary.com

Copyright © 2016 Jump!
International copyright reserved in all countries.
No part of this book may be reproduced in any form
without written permission from the publisher.

Library of Congress Cataloging-in-Publication Data

Pettiford, Rebecca, author.
  Harvesting / by Rebecca Pettiford.
    pages cm. – (Way to grow! Gardening)
  Includes index.
  ISBN 978-1-62031-230-8 (hardcover: alk. paper) –
  ISBN 978-1-62496-317-9 (ebook)
  1. Harvesting–Juvenile literature. I. Title. II. Series:
  Pettiford, Rebecca. Way to grow! Gardening.
  SB129.P495 2015
  631.5'5–dc23
                                        2015000297

Series Editor: Jenny Fretland VanVoorst
Series Designer: Anna Peterson
Photo Researcher: Anna Peterson

Photo Credits: All photos by Shutterstock except:
age fotostock, 11; Dreamstime, 8-9, 10; Getty, 5, 12-13,
16-17; Thinkstock, 20-21, 23.

Printed in the United States of America at
Corporate Graphics in North Mankato, Minnesota.

TABLE OF CONTENTS

CHAPTER 1

HARVESTING YOUR PLANTS

You worked in your garden all spring and summer. Now it's time to **harvest** your plants.

How do you know when to cut your flowers?

How do you know when to pick the berries and pull up the carrots? Let's find out!

CHAPTER 2

FLOWERS

Do you want fresh flowers for a vase? Gather flowers in the morning before it gets hot.

Try to cut them before
the blooms are fully open.
They will open in water.

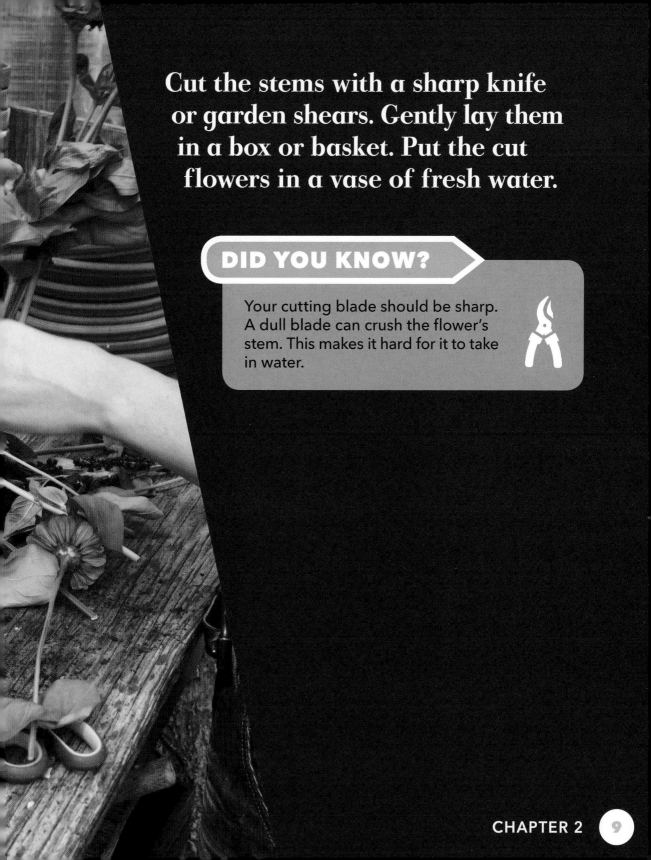

Cut the stems with a sharp knife or garden shears. Gently lay them in a box or basket. Put the cut flowers in a vase of fresh water.

DID YOU KNOW?

Your cutting blade should be sharp. A dull blade can crush the flower's stem. This makes it hard for it to take in water.

CHAPTER 3

FRUITS AND VEGETABLES

Look at the fruits and vegetables in your garden. Are the colors bright?

If they look good enough to eat,
they are often ready to pick!

Pick berries and grapes when they are fully **ripe**. They should come off the plant easily.

Pick fruits like oranges and cherries when they are ripe on the tree.

You can pick other tree fruits just before they are ripe. Pears, peaches, plums, and mangoes will all continue to ripen inside.

For the best taste, gather most vegetables before a **frost**. But some vegetables can handle a bit of cold weather.

In the case of Brussels sprouts, cabbage, and kale, frost actually improves the flavor!

TAKE A LOOK!

Fruits and vegetables go through four stages between planting and harvesting.

1. seedling   2. leaf stage

3. flower stage   4. fruit stage

You can leave many **root vegetables** in the ground during the winter. However, they must have a heavy layer of **mulch** on top of them.

mulch

Vegetables like garlic, onions, and **winter squash** must be **cured** after you pick them.

What does that mean?

It means storing them in warm, dry air. This will make their skin hard. It will keep their insides from rotting.

DID YOU KNOW?

Thanksgiving is a harvest festival. **Kwanzaa** is, too. These festivals are a time for us to give thanks for the food we have gathered.

Fruit and vegetables taste best eaten at the peak of ripeness. Flowers are prettiest in full bloom. But it's up to you to get them there.

You must give your plants the right mix of sun, soil, water, and loving care. Then your harvest will be worth celebrating!

ACTIVITIES & TOOLS

BAKE CARROT CHIPS

You can use carrots harvested from your garden to make sweet chips!

What You Need:

- an oven (Never use the oven without adult help.)
- vegetable peeler
- two carrots
- 2 tsp. (10 milliliters) olive oil
- 2 tsp. (10 ml) honey
- salt and pepper
- baking sheet

❶ **Preheat the oven to 350 degrees Fahrenheit (177 degrees Celsius).**

❷ **Use a vegetable peeler to thinly slice two carrots.**

❸ **Toss carrot slices with olive oil, honey, and a little salt and pepper.**

❹ **Place the carrot slices in a single layer on the baking sheet. Cook for 10 minutes.**

❺ **Turn them over. Cook for another 10 minutes.**

❻ **Enjoy!**

GLOSSARY

cure: To preserve or save vegetables by storing them in dry air.

frost: A freezing temperature.

harvest: To gather crops such as flowers, fruits, and vegetables.

Kwanzaa: An African-American cultural festival held from December 26 to January 1.

mulch: Dead leaves or wood chips that you spread around a plant to help the soil.

ripe: Fully grown and developed.

root vegetables: Vegetables that grow under the ground.

winter squash: A squash, like pumpkin or acorn squash, that has a hard skin.

INDEX

TO LEARN MORE

Learning more is as easy as 1, 2, 3.

1) Go to www.factsurfer.com

2) Enter "harvesting" into the search box.

3) Click the "Surf" to see a list of websites.

With factsurfer, finding more information is just a click away.